SPIRITUAL ENC

Entering God's Presence

Stephen D. Eyre

A Month
of
Guided
Quiet
Times

InterVarsity Press
DOWNERS GROVE, ILLINOIS 60515

To David and Nancy Moore, those with whom I've entered the presence of God.

InterVarsity Press is the book-publishing division of InterVarsity Christian Fellowship, a student movement active on campus at hundreds of universities, colleges and schools of nursing in the United States of America, and a member movement of the International Fellowship of Evangelical Students. For information about local and regional activities, write Public Relations Dept., InterVarsity Christian Fellowship, 6400 Schroeder Rd., P.O. Box 7895, Madison, WI 53707-7895.

Cover photograph: Peter French

ISBN 0-8308-1176-1

Printed in the United States of America

16 15 14 13 12 11 10 9 8 7 6 5 4 3 2 1
05 04 03 02 01 00 99 98 97 96 95 94 93 92

Introduction

The unbelief of our age creates clouds of spiritual darkness. It penetrates even to the hearts of committed Christians. We can have a sense of devotion to God but then slowly, quietly slip away from God as the One we know, so that he becomes One we merely know about.

We need to do something.

Prayer and Bible study are the mainstay of any spiritual diet. But we must be alert. Our need to be productive Christians can lead us to do too much, too fast and in the wrong way. Instead of worshiping in the presence of God, we can barge in, tell God what to do and how to do it, read over a couple of Scriptures for inspiration, and then rush off to get on with life. This approach won't get us very far. It robs God of our praise and deprives us of spiritual nourishment.

Spiritual Exercises

As a teenager, my older brother was determined to become a pilot in the Air Force. However, when he took his physical, he discovered that he was not qualified. His eyesight was not good enough.

He spent a day or two in depression, and then decided to see what he could do about it. Eventually, an eye doctor gave him a set of slightly out of focus picture-cards to look at. My brother was to stare at the cards until he could bring the pictures into focus. After a month or two of these exercises, he took the test again and passed.

Similarly, if we sense that our spiritual sight is dull or out of focus, we can do something about it. That is what spiritual exercises are for.

For the past several years I have been meeting with students and business people to seek God and have quiet times together. Seeking to make spiritual exercises personal and practical, I make suggestions about ways to approach God. We worship and pray for a while, and then we talk. I have come to call these sessions "guided quiet times."

I have taken the substance of these guided quiet times and put them into a month-long course of study. Their purpose is two-fold: to encourage you in fellowship with God, and to provide skills that will become lifelong disciplines.

Part One: Warming Up to God

We live in a world consumed with activity. The pace leaves us stretched and sluggish toward God. Martin Luther believed in a period of warming up as we approach God. In his letter *A Simple Way to Pray, for a Good Friend* Luther speaks of "warming the heart," getting the heart to come to itself, waiting until the heart "gets in the mood." If it was necessary in the sixteenth century, which has been called the *Age of Faith,* how much more do we need a warming up period in this age of unbelief.

During this first week, we will look at what it means to desire God, ways that we resist God, and how to become quiet inside so that we can face God and worship him.

Part Two: Studying and Meditating on Scripture

When our hearts are warm, Scripture becomes the fuel that feeds the spiritual flame of knowledge. However, a proper handling of Scripture requires effort, time and skill. We need to soak in a passage, to read, study and meditate on it, until it becomes a part of us. So for the entire week we will spend time in Psalm 34.

Part Three: Meditating on Life

God is here and is active in our world. But we must look at life through Scripture to recognize him. We can miss him unless we look—hard.

In part three we will learn to use Scripture as spectacles to ponder God's hand in the course of our lives. Along with Scripture, we will get in touch with our emotions. While emotions can be abused, they are nevertheless indispensable for living in the presence of God. Then, we will look at God's hand in the past, the present and the future.

Part Four: Praying

Prayer is the ultimate privilege. What could be greater than to ask God for something and have him do it? But we often pray for too much, too quickly. Prayer is a weighty privilege and used improperly it can exhaust us spiritually.

In part four we will consider the type of prayers that God answers. What should we pray for? How can we know we are praying properly? We will practice knowing that biblical prayer comes from hearts that have life by the Spirit, which are shaped by the Scriptures and which are enriched by meditation.

Guidelines

You will find each of the four elements, approaching God, study and meditation on Scripture, meditation on the events of life and prayer, woven into this guide. Some days you will have all four elements, some days just two or three. By the end of your study you will have experienced a pattern of quiet times that you can use on your own.

Approach	Study
Reflect	Pray

How much time is required for each day? Each session is designed to last about half an hour, although you could spend a great deal more time if you wanted to.

And while the guided times are written so that they can all be covered in a month, you might find it necessary and profitable to spread them out over a couple months. The subjects covered are meant to introduce you to different spiritual exercises. You may want to work on one exercise for a couple of days before moving on to the next.

If possible, choose a partner or two to have quiet time with. Sharing these times together will bring a deeper spiritual enrichment. You might want to meet at a set time, work through the assignment together, and then share. Or perhaps you might want to work through several days individually, and then meet together once or twice a week to share.

Caution: this study guide is not intended to make you feel guilty. Some people will go through the guide daily in a month—and find it is easy to do so. If so, great! Others will find it difficult.

I am one who struggles to discipline myself to work through any guide. If you are like me, keep yourself moving. If you have decided you want to use it, don't let it go for weeks without touching it. But don't condemn yourself if you miss a few days here and there.

Knowing God

A Christian leader of a previous generation, A.W. Tozer, has been an inspiration to me in the pursuit of God. The following is the last paragraph of his preface in *The Pursuit of God:*

> This book is a modest attempt to aid God's hungry children so to find him. Nothing here is new except in the sense that it is a discovery which my own heart has made of spiritual realities most delightful and wonderful to me. Others before me have gone much farther into these holy mysteries than I have done, but if my fire is not large it is yet real, and there may be those who can light their candle at its flame. (Send the Light, 1987)

WEEK 1

Warming Up to God

Clap your hands, all you nations;
shout to God with cries of joy.
How awesome is the LORD Most High,
the great King over all the earth!
He subdued nations under us,
peoples under our feet.
He chose our inheritance for us,
the pride of Jacob, whom he loved.

God has ascended amid shouts of joy,
the LORD amid the sounding of trumpets.
Sing praises to God, sing praises;
sing praises to our King, sing praises.

For God is the King of all the earth;
sing to him a psalm of praise.
God reigns over the nations;
God is seated on his holy throne.
The nobles of the nations assemble
as the people of the God of Abraham,
for the kings of the earth belong to God;
he is greatly exalted. (Ps 47)

DAY 1

Desiring God

My soul thirsts for God, for the living God.
When can I go and meet with God? (Ps 42:2)

Spiritual good is of a satisfying nature. . . . And the more a man experiences this . . . satisfying sweetness, the more earnestly will he hunger and thirst for more. (Jonathan Edwards, Religious Affections *[Banner of Truth, 1986], p. 305)*

There is something deep within us that longs for God. It is the inner work of God's Spirit that all God's children have. We have a divinely given desire to seek him out and enjoy his presence. The famous Westminster Confession, written in the seventeenth century puts it this way, "The chief end of man and woman is to glorify God and to enjoy him forever."

But, that inner hunger can grow weak unless it is nourished and cultivated. Preoccupation with day-to-day living can choke it out. If you are a student, it may be a concern about grades or finding the right partner. If you are earning a living or raising a family, it may be balancing the budget or moving up the corporate ladder. Jesus rebuked the church at Ephesus for having lost their burning desire. "Yet I hold this against you: You have forsaken your first love" (Rev 2:4).

As we begin this course of spiritual study, let us be clear that the first requirement for spiritual health is a strong inner desire for God. A. W. Tozer writes:

> Come near to the holy men and women of the past and you will soon feel the heat of their desire after God. They mourned for Him, they prayed and wrestled and sought for Him day and night, in season and out, and when they found Him, the finding was all the

sweeter for the long seeking. (A. W. Tozer, *The Pursuit of God* [Send the Light], 1987)

Unless there is an inner desire for God all the praying, good works and Bible study are merely empty shells.

Approach

This morning as you begin, ask God to fan the sparks of love for him into a healthy, crackling fire. Consider how much you have felt a desire for God recently.

Study

Look up these verses to see how important it is to desire God. As you look them up, ask God to speak them to your heart. Then write out in your own words what each one says.

Psalm 27:4, 8:

Psalm 62:1:

Psalm 63 (especially verses 1, 5, 8):

Psalm 84 (especially verses 1-2):

Jeremiah 29:11-14:

Matthew 13:44-46:

Reflect

From what you have read and from your own experience list reasons you can think of why it is important to hunger after God.

Try to recall times when you enjoyed a strong hunger for the Lord. This may have been times in fellowship with other believers, or it may have been in a quiet walk on the road. List a few of them.

Pray

Spend time now seeking God to give you a heart that longs for him. Pray that God would do the same for your family and fellow Christians.

Pray about other concerns that you need to lift up to God.

DAY 2

Resisting God

Where can I go from your Spirit?
Where can I flee from your presence? (Ps 139:7)

While there is something deep within us that longs for God, we sometimes avoid him as well. Yet, it is not easy to see how we resist God. After all, aren't Christians supposed to want to be with God?

During a session of spiritual guidance that I was involved with, a young woman came face-to-face with her avoidance:

> "I'm not sure what I am upset about, but I know it has to do with the way I see God," she said. "I realized that I keep God at a distance. I want to know him, but I don't. It's like Jesus is standing at the door of my life and I have it open just a crack. If I open it all the way, I am sure that he is going to burst in and tell me I have to be a nun. I hope that if I can just keep his laws and don't look at him directly, then maybe I can still live my life the way I want to." (Stephen Eyre, *Defeating the Dragons of the World* [Downers Grove, Ill.: InterVarsity Press, 1987], p. 127)

There are numerous reasons for avoiding God. Several common ones are:

☐ We feel guilty and are afraid to face him.
☐ We are disappointed by him.
☐ We are angry at him and feel like he has let us down.

☐ We are afraid that he will make what we think are unreasonable demands on us.

Because we are masters of self-deception, it is easy to avoid God and not even be aware of it.

One of my personal patterns of avoidance is the "just a minute" syndrome. When I sit down to read Scripture, my eye will catch a magazine article that I want to read. I put down my Bible to read the article, telling myself I'll get back to the Scriptures in just a couple of minutes. But somehow I never do.

Another of my patterns is the "I'm too busy" syndrome. I can go a couple of weeks without an extended time with the Lord. Initially, my excuse is that there is too much to do today, and I'll get to it tomorrow. But the "tomorrow" turns out to be a couple of weeks. When that happens, I know that I am avoiding meeting with God.

Approach

Make a list of things that are on your mind that come between you and him right now. Lift each one up to the Lord and ask him to take them.

Study

Let's look at the principle of avoidance from Scripture. Read Genesis 3:6-10. In your own words, briefly describe what happened.

In response to God's question, "Where are you?" Adam responds, "I was afraid because I was naked; so I hid." What was wrong with Adam being naked?

What emotions do you think Adam and Eve might have experienced when God came to them in the Garden?

Jesus confronted religious leaders who appeared to be seeking God, but in fact were not. Mark 7:6 says: "He replied, 'Isaiah was right when he prophesied about you hypocrites; as it is written: "These people honor me with their lips, but their hearts are far from me." ' " What is Jesus' point in this passage?

Reflect

How would you feel if God showed up to go on an afternoon walk with you today?

Like the Pharisees, we can appear to be seeking God when in fact we are avoiding him. How do you compare to the Pharisees in your pursuit of God?

If we are to grow spiritually we must be able to discern the ways in which we personally avoid God, and know what to do about it. Where do you see patterns of ingrained avoidance of God going on in your own life?

God called Adam and Eve out of hiding. How do you sense God may be calling you out of hiding to meet with him?

What difference do you think it would make in your life if you stopped avoiding him?

Pray

You need God's help to see the patterns of behavior you use to hide from him. Ask God to show you.

Ask him to free you and release your heart to continue to grow in seeking him.

Pray that your family and fellow Christians throughout the world would unreservedly seek him.

DAY 3

Settling in God's Presence

My heart is not proud, O LORD,
my eyes are not haughty;
I do not concern myself with great matters
or things too wonderful for me.
But I have stilled and quieted my soul;
like a weaned child with its mother,
like a weaned child is my soul within me.
O Israel, put your hope in the LORD
both now and forevermore. (Ps 131)

We live in a busy world. And we are busy people. But if we are going to spend time with God, we will have to slow down our pace. We have to stop doing things all the time so that we can create a space in our lives to be with God. You have already begun to do this by working your way through this guide.

But you will discover that stopping outwardly is not enough.

Once I have stopped outwardly, I discover that I am still busy inwardly. My mind is full of things I need to do, or should have done. People to phone, letters to write, errands to run. The list is endless. If I am going to meet God, then I have to get past these inner demands to sit worshipfully in his presence.

How can we become still—inwardly and outwardly?

First, don't ignore the demands upon you. It is because they are important to you that they have such power. Richard Foster writes:

> We can give up the need to watch out for number one because we have One who is watching out for us. I sometimes like to picture a box in which I place every worry and every care. When it is full I gift wrap it, placing a lovely big bow on top and give it as a present to the Father. He receives it, and once he does I know I must not

take it back, for to take back a gift once given is most discourteous. (Richard Foster, *Meditative Prayer* [Downers Grove, Ill.: InterVarsity Press, 1985])

Approach

However we do it, we need to give over our concerns to the Lord. Let's begin by writing out a list of pressing issues on a "to do" list. (After you have spent time in the study you will come back to it in the reflection time.)

Study

Read the following Scriptures:

Be still before the LORD and wait patiently for him;
do not fret when men succeed in their ways,
when they carry out their wicked schemes. (Ps 37:7)

Be still, and know that I am God;

I will be exalted among the nations,
I will be exalted in the earth. (Ps 46:10)

What do we need to know if we are to be still?

Why is it important to be still?

Read Exodus 14:13-18. How was Israel still and active at the same time?

What was God's role in the deliverance of Israel?

What were the people supposed to do?

Reflect

As you sit before the Lord, consider the list you made. Following Richard Foster's suggestions, see yourself standing before the Lord. Put the list in a box and make a gift of it to the Lord.

Consider what happened as you went through the giving over exercise. Were you able to do it or did you resist?

How did the Lord respond to you when you presented the box to him?

How do you feel after so specifically taking your cares to him?

What difference will this make in the way you face today?

Pray

Pray through your list. Ask God for wisdom on each one. Ask him to protect you from taking them back.

DAY 4

Listening to God

This is my Son, whom I love. Listen to him! (Mk 9:7)

I have other sheep that are not of this sheep pen. . . .
They too will listen to my voice. (Jn 10:16)

If we want a personal encounter with God, then we must not only stop being so busy, we must also stop talking so much at God when we pray.

It is easy to think of prayer as a monologue. "God please do this, please take care of that." But a monologue is boring to the person who is forced to listen and exhausting to the person who feels a need to keep up the unceasing flow of words.

Today, you are going to take a different approach. Resist telling God to do anything. Spend your quiet time asking God questions and then sit in expectation to hear what he will say.

> Speak, Lord, for I, Your servant am ready to hear You. . . . The children of Israel said to Moses: Speak to us and we will hear you, but let the Lord not speak to us, lest perhaps we die for dread. Not so, Lord, not so, I beseech You. Rather I ask humbly with Samuel the prophet that you speak to me Yourself. . . . (Thomas à Kempis, *The Imitation of Christ* [Hodder & Stoughton, 1979])

Approach

As you did yesterday, turn everything over to the Lord. Write down how you feel after you have done it.

Study

Read Habakkuk 2:1-3. What does Habakkuk say to God verse 1, and how does God respond, verses 2-3?

What was required of Habakkuk to be ready to hear the Lord?

Read Psalm 32:8-9. Ponder God's promise of instruction. What is required of those he speaks to?

Reflect

God promises to guide us and speak to our concerns. Do you expect him to instruct you? Explain.

The Scriptures are God's written word to us. Write down what it is like to be guided by his Word.

To help yourself learn to listen, make a list of questions and concerns you would like God to address.

Ask God what he thinks about your problem with. . . . Ask God what he wants you to do about. . . . Sit back and wait quietly to see what God will say.

Does it seem strange to actually listen for God to talk back? John Powell writes:

> The Lord . . . puts his ideas into my mind and especially his perspectives. He widens my vision, helps me to see what is really important in life, and to distinguish the really important from the unimportant. . . . He comes to me in the listening, receptive moments of prayer, and he transfuses his power into me. (As quoted in Joyce Huggett, *The Joy of Listening to God* [Downers Grove, Ill.: InterVarsity Press, 1986])

What did you learn from this experience?

Pray

Tell God that you want to grow in the ability to discern his voice. Pray the prayer of Thomas à Kempis at the beginning of this study.

DAY 5

Resting in God

The Lord is my shepherd, I shall lack nothing.
He makes me lie down in green pastures,
he leads me beside quiet waters,
he restores my soul. (Ps 23:1-2)

After we have stopped being busy inwardly, after we have stopped telling God how to run our lives—and the world—there is a full, resting, quiet that we can enter into.

When you have reached this stage, you can just sit back and enjoy being with the Lord. You don't have to do anything. Joyce Huggett describes it like this:

> What I heard in those times of listening was more than a voice. It was a presence. Yes. I heard the Lord call my name. But I also 'heard' his tenderness. I soaked up his love. Sometimes it seemed as though Jesus himself stood in front of me or beside me or above me. . . . The only way I can describe it is to liken it to the overwhelming a person feels when they love someone very deeply. . . . No words are necessary. They might even be intrusive, for they could trivialize the love. (Joyce Huggett, *Joy*)

Approach

Sit quietly for a few moments. If you can enter into the silence described above, write down a few words to describe it. If you can't enter silence yet write down the distractions that you feel and give them over to the Lord.

Study

Read the following verses:

> My soul finds rest in God alone;
> my salvation comes from him.
> He alone is my rock and my salvation;
> he is my fortress, I will never be shaken. (Ps 62:1-2)

Why does the author say that he has a sense of inner rest?

How do the qualities of God he mentions offer us rest?

Read 1 Chronicles 22:9-13. The blessing of God to David and all Israel was to give them rest and peace through the rulership of Solomon. List ways in which Solomon foreshadows a glimpse of the ministry of the lordship of Jesus Christ for all Christians, especially for you.

Reflect

In what ways have you ever experienced God as a rock and a fortress?

Who in your life has God sent to be his agent of rest and peace?

God intends his day of worship to be a day of rest. And likewise, our times of worship daily should be times of rest as well. As you enter into a time of worship and rest with the Lord today, don't write anymore. Sit back and relax. God is with you and you are with him. In his presence there is nothing that you need to do.

After you have spent a resting time with the Lord, write down what it was like. (How did you feel? What did you enjoy? Was there something that made you uncomfortable?)

Pray

Ask God to give you faith to increase your trust of him as your rock and fortress.

Ask God to give you people in your life that can be his agents of rest and peace.

DAY 6

Repenting before God

For I know my transgressions,
and my sin is always before me. (Ps 51:3)

But now in Christ Jesus you who once were far away have been brought near through the blood of Christ. (Eph 2:13)

It's satisfying to be near God. But as we draw close to him, we face the problem of our sinfulness. Even when we seek to please God, we discover how much we fall short. This feels bad because we don't like to disappoint those we love.

For several years I read the Sermon on the Mount daily. Time after time I discovered that I could not meet Jesus' standard as I measured myself against the demands of inner righteousness of the sermon. Each morning, as I came to him, I found myself embarrassed. "Lord, I have done it again." Daily I had to repent.

When I first discovered the necessity of daily repentance, I felt foolish. Was I the only Christian who was so spiritually weak? Sometime later, however, I discovered, and took comfort, in the words of Martin Luther. Number one of Luther's famous "Ninety-five Theses" is "When our Lord and Master Jesus Christ said, 'Repent,' he willed that the entire life of believers to be one of repentance" (Timothy George, *Theology of the Reformers* [Nashville: Broadman, 1988], p. 48).

For those of us who seek God, repentance must be a lifestyle.

But beyond that, and this too can be quite difficult, we must believe that we are received, despite our sin, through the blood of Jesus Christ.

Approach

Ask God to give you the courage to face your sin.

Make a list of the things that you feel badly or guilty about as you draw near to God.

Study

Read from Jesus' Sermon on the Mount, Matthew 5:21-48. How do you compare with his standard of righteousness?

Comparing our heart motivation with the Lord's standards is very sobering. Now read Romans 7:21—8:12. Describe the battle that the apostle Paul is struggling with.

How does he feel about his inclination toward sin?

What hope does he have for dealing with it?

Reflect

How do you see a battle with sin in your own life?

How do you feel about your own inclination to sin?

Apply the cross and the gift of Jesus' righteousness to your sin. How does it feel to be forgiven?

Pray

Ask God to give you the courage to face your sin and the boldness to repent.

Ask God to increase your gratitude for the gift of forgiveness in Christ.

DAY 7

Being Devoted to God

Sing joyfully to the LORD, you righteous;
it is fitting for the upright to praise him.
Praise the LORD with the harp;
make music to him on the ten-stringed lyre.
Sing to him a new song;
play skillfully, and shout for joy. (Ps 33:1-3)

The sign of a spiritually healthy heart is gratitude and affection. You will discover that after you have spent time in spiritual exercises there rises from within the heart a deep sense of gratitude. Galatians 4:6 says, "Because you are sons, God sent the Spirit of his Son into our hearts, the Spirit who calls out, 'Abba, Father.' " We can actually sense the Spirit within us as he cries, "Abba, Father."

Allow your affection for God to rise up within you. To be with God is to be with the One who is life, health, joy, beauty. When we draw near to him, how can we help but worship him?

But drawing near in your heart takes time and maturity. You may not have come far enough in your preparation of being with the Lord for the voice of gratitude to rise within you as a way of life.

> Many people try to come into joy far too soon. Often we try to pump up people with joy when in reality nothing has happened in their lives. God has not broken into the routine experiences of their daily existence. (Richard Foster, *Celebration of Discipline* [San Francisco: Harper & Row, rev. ed., 1989], p. 166)

Approach

Make a list of things you are thankful for.

While you may not be able to express gratitude right now, if you continue to walk in this inner spiritual pilgrimage, it will come in time. If you do feel gratitude, sit for awhile in heartfelt thanks to God.

Study

Read Psalm 47. What is the psalmist thankful for?

What actions of joy and gratitude do you see in these verses?

Read Psalm 66. What is the psalmist thankful for?

How does the psalmist express his joy?

Reflect

How would you feel using the same outward expressions of joy as the psalmist?

The psalmist sings, claps, sacrifices and invites others to share in his joy in God. What ways can you outwardly show your joy in the Lord?

The Holy Spirit within us is continually offering praise. If you can, allow yourself to join the Spirit in praise. Try to write a psalm to the Lord, including in it reasons you enjoy knowing God. If you haven't come to the place of heartfelt worship, don't try to generate what you don't feel. You might want to sing a song or hymn that you can sing with meaning. Or perhaps play some recorded music that reflects your mood.

Pray

Ask God to give you the courage to walk in honesty until he brings you into the place of inner praise.

WEEK 2

Studying and Meditating on Scripture

I will extol the LORD at all times;
his praise will always be on my lips.
My soul will boast in the LORD;
let the afflicted hear and rejoice.
Glorify the LORD with me;
let us exalt his name together.

I sought the LORD, and he answered me;
he delivered me from all my fears.
Those who look to him are radiant;
their faces are never covered with shame.
This poor man called, and the LORD heard him;
he saved him out of all his troubles.
The angel of the LORD encamps around those who fear him,
and he delivers them.

Taste and see that the LORD is good;
blessed is the man who takes refuge in him.
Fear the LORD, you his saints,
for those who fear him lack nothing.
The lions may grow weak and hungry,
but those who seek the LORD lack no good thing. (Ps 34:1-10)

DAY 8
Reading the Scriptures

Open my eyes that I may see
wonderful things in your law. (Ps 119:18)

If we are going to know God, we must desire him. And if we are going to desire him, we must have our hearts warmed by his Word. When we seek to know God through his Scriptures, we are not only looking for principles to live by, but also personal truth to nourish our souls.

The spiritual growth that comes from reading the Scriptures requires effort on our part. We need to read, study and think about Scripture. This requires that we use our minds to the fullest. Warm hearts come from well-developed minds.

> Holy affections are not heat without light; but evermore arise from the information of the understanding. . . . Knowledge is the key that first opens the hard heart, and enlarges the affections, and so opens the way for men into the kingdom of heaven. (Jonathan Edwards, *Religious Affections,* p. 192)

We can't be casual about the Scriptures. Just as we can eat poorly, grabbing a sandwich on the run, we can read Scripture poorly. We may read a passage from the Gospels one day, a couple of verses from Psalms the next, and jump to the epistles on the next. That alone is not a healthy way to read Scripture. While we may draw rich nuggets of truth this way, we won't learn to see the broader message that God gave to each author.

It is important to choose a portion of the Bible and soak in it. So for this week we will choose Psalm 34. First, we will read it, then study it, and then meditate on it. Finally, we will apply it.

Approach

Sit quietly for a few minutes. Give over your cares to the Lord one by one so that you have a sense of resting in the Lord.

Study

Turn to Psalm 34 and read it. Write down briefly what you think it said.

Write down which verses seem to group together naturally. Give a brief title to them.

What can you tell about the character of David the author from this psalm?

Reflect

What in these verses entices your interest in the Lord?

What in these verses expresses what you need to desire from God?

With Psalm 34 open in front of you spend some time in worship. Lift up your heart and open it to God. (It might help you to actually picture in your mind's eye a door on your heart. Put your hand on the door, open it up and invite the Lord in.) Tell God what you like about him.

Tell him how you feel about him.

Pray

Ask God to teach you his Word and to strengthen your Bible study skills.

DAY 9

Learning to Observe

I have hidden your word in my heart
that I might not sin against you.
Praise be to you, O LORD;
teach me your decrees. (Ps 119:11-12)

Reading a passage once is not enough to cause us to hide it in our hearts. We need to read it again and again to grasp how it can shape us. Richard Foster writes:

> When we study a book of the Bible we are seeking to be controlled by the intent of the author. We are determined to hear what he is saying, not what we would like him to say. We are willing to pay the price of barren day after barren day until the meaning is clear. This process revolutionizes our life. (Richard Foster, *Celebration*, p. 60)

We will never be able to embrace the truth of a passage in our hearts unless we know what was important to the author as he wrote it. King David wrote Psalm 34 after he had escaped being chased by a Gentile king named Abimelech. Today, we are going to find out some of the things that were on David's mind as he wrote it.

Approach

Spiritually, emotionally or physically we can feel like spending time with God is merely a chore. Everybody feels that way sometimes. Choose to do it because it's right. We will reap great benefits from such faithfulness. Spend time now setting your heart to seek God.

Study

One key to unlocking any passage is to look for repeated words or ideas. In order to do this you will have to read Psalm 34 several times, keeping in mind that you want to find the central idea. As you read, jot down repeated words or ideas.

Another key to understanding a passage is to look for *who* is mentioned. *What* people (or type of people) are referred to? (For instance what do you find out about the righteous? the wicked? the Lord?)

A third key to understanding a passage is to look for *what is happening* or what is required. Try to find out what David says is required of those who receive the Lord's care.

Reflect
Spend some time evaluating your own life in light of what you have discovered today.

Pray
Ask God to apply these truths to your heart.

Ask him to give you perseverance to grow in Bible knowledge and study skills.

DAY 10

Interpreting the Scriptures

Let me understand the teaching of your precepts;
then I will meditate on your wonders. (Ps 119:27)

Now that you have looked at the passage a couple of times, you are getting closer to meditating on it. But you are not ready yet.

There is more work to be done because it is possible to read a passage and never know what it means. Not only do you have to read a passage several times, you have to think about it—a lot. We all have had the experience of struggling to understand something until finally the light of understanding breaks in, "Of course, now I see what that means!"

> Spiritually to understand the Scriptures is to have the eyes of the mind opened to behold the wonderful spiritual excellency of the glorious things contained in the true meaning of it, and that always were contained in it, ever since it was written. (Jonathan Edwards, *Religious Affections*, p. 206)

Today, you need to think about some of the key ideas of Psalm 34, seeking to understand what they mean.

Study

Read Psalm 34. What do *extol, praise, boast* and *glorify* mean in verses 1-

3? Use a dictionary and look up each word.

Compare them. How are they similar?

How are they different?

Look at verse 8. What does it mean to taste and see that the Lord is good?

Look over verses 11-14. What does it mean to fear the Lord?

What benefits come to the righteous (vv. 15-22)? Make a list.

Reflect

You looked up several different words for praise. Spend time worshiping the Lord using what you have learned.

What is the difference between the fear of the Lord that David writes of and being fearful of God's presence the way Adam and Eve were?

How can you benefit by growing in the fear of the Lord?

David wasn't afraid of God because he knew the gift of God's righteousness. As Christians, we know we become righteous through faith in Jesus Christ. Conclude your time by thinking about what Paul wrote to the Christians at Rome in Romans 1:17: "For in the gospel a righteousness from God is revealed, a righteousness that is by faith from first to last, just as it is written: 'The righteous will live by faith.' "

Pray

Seek God for your needs and the needs of your friends.

Ask God to give growing insight into the meaning of Scripture.

DAY 11

Reflecting on the Scriptures

Reflect on what I am saying, for the Lord will give you insight into all this. (2 Tim 2:7)

For several years I tried to get my family to have Sherlock Holmes as a reading project. (A family reading project in our house means that I read and they listen.) After we moved to England, everyone became interested because there was a sense of familiarity about it. As we read, we all marveled at Holmes's ability to pick up clues and come up with what really happened. He walks around asking questions, looks at seemingly insignificant details, and then wanders off to think about it. And, of course, from these seemingly useless tidbits of information he is able to solve the crime.

There is a principle of reflection involved in Holmes's method. We must look closely at details. But that is not enough. Having looked up close, we need to stand back and take it all in. We need to be able to put pieces together. That's what reflection is all about—thinking about something until everything fits.

The process of reflection is important in biblical meditation as well:

> Reflection brings us to see things from God's perspective. . . . When we ponder the meaning of what we study, we come to hear and see things in a new way. . . . It soon becomes obvious that study demands humility. It can not happen until we are willing to submit to the subject matter. (Richard Foster, *Celebration*, p. 57)

You are now becoming familiar with what Psalm 34 is all about. You have looked at some of the key ideas. Now it's time to step back and ponder the whole psalm.

Study

Read the whole psalm again. Summarize the main point of the psalm in one or two brief sentences.

God is the subject of the psalm. Describe David's view of God.

David makes some pretty sweeping statements about the certainty of God's deliverance. How could he say such things with such certainty? Base your response on several verses.

Reflect

What influence does David want this psalm to make on those who read it?

How is this psalm beginning to affect you?

What needs or dangers are you facing from which you need deliverance or protection?

How have you experienced the Lord's protection and deliverance in the past?

Pray

Call out for the Lord to be with you in the tasks that you face today.

Ask God to bring back Psalm 34 to mind throughout your day so you can be constantly nourished by its truth.

DAY 12

Seeing the Scriptures

Do not let this Book of the Law depart from your mouth; meditate on it day and night, so that you may be careful to do everything written in it. Then you will be prosperous and successful. (Josh 1:8)

When we meditate on Scripture, we seek not only to have the Word of God enter our hearts, but we also seek to enter into the Scriptures. First, we try to find out everything we can about it. That is what we have been doing in our quiet times in Psalm 34 this week. Once we have studied it, then it is time to enter into it through the use of our mind's eye.

> Francis de Sales has instructed us to ". . . represent to your imagination the whole mystery on which you desire to meditate as if it is really in your presence. For example, if you wish to meditate on our Lord on the Cross, imagine that you are on Mount Calvary, and that you there behold and hear all that was done or said on the day of the passion." (Richard Foster, *Celebration*, p. 26)

Approach

Sit back and get comfortable. Spend some time getting quiet, perhaps going through the exercise of making a list of all your needs. Now turn over to God all the concerns that you are facing today. See yourself handing them to God.

Study

Now read through Psalm 34.

Enter into the celebration of God. The depth of David's danger is expressed in the exaltation of his deliverance. David calls his people to celebrate God as the delivering conqueror. Imagine yourself in the center of a victory celebration where the hero is being praised for his powerful leadership.

Perhaps you will see yourself with troops around the campfire recounting the victory. Perhaps you will see yourself in a huge palace with a great spread of food. Create your own picture and celebrate God. (However, remember that our pictures of God are always limited. Never let them become images or idols that you live by.)

Experience the relief of deliverance from danger. Because this psalm is about deliverance from danger, look through the psalm and pick out verses that mention danger. Picture what David must have felt like when he was in trouble. Imagine that you are there with him.

What do you see, hear, smell?

Twice David mentions a refuge in the Lord (vv. 8 and 27). Think of a strong safe place to hide from trouble. That's how David viewed the Lord. What does it feel like to be in a safe place protected from threats on the outside?

There is no self-reliance in this psalm. David looked to the Lord for deliverance, not depending on his outstanding skill as a soldier.

Again, see yourself with David in a threatening situation and the Lord being just the protection that you need. Rest in the strength of the spiritual forces that surround you. Verse 7 speaks of the angel of the Lord encamping with an army around those who need help. Picture yourself surrounded by spiritual forces which can protect you from danger.

Reflect

After you have spent time entering into Psalm 34, summarize how it has affected you.

Pray

Ask God to make his righteousness and justice known throughout the world.

Ask God to give you eyes to see him in the Scriptures and in your daily tasks.

DAY 13

Meeting God

Then their eyes were opened and they recognized him,
and he disappeared from their sight. They asked each other,
"Were not our hearts burning within us while he talked
with us on the road and opened the Scriptures to us?" (Lk 24:31-32)

The disciples' hearts burned as they saw Jesus and heard him explain the Scriptures. They had been with him for hours, and yet they didn't recognize him. Likewise, we can read a passage over and over again, and miss the Lord who is the subject of all Scripture.

One of the spiritual disciplines of church history is *lectio divina,* or "divine reading." It means seeking to read Scripture with a heart of devotion in order to be with the Lord. Basil Pennington describes it this way:

> It is not a question of reading a paragraph, a page or a chapter. It is, rather sitting down with a friend, the Lord and letting him speak to us. We listen. And if what he says in the first word of the sentence strikes us, we stop and let it sink in. We relish it. We respond from our heart. We enjoy it to the full before we move on. There is no hurry. We are sitting with our friend. . . . We let him speak. We really listen. (As quoted in Joyce Huggett, *Joy*)

Martin Luther used to speak of his thoughts taking a walk with the Lord.

> When such rich good thoughts come, one should let the other prayers go and give room to these thoughts, listen to them in silence and by no means suppress them. For here the Holy Spirit himself

is preaching, and one word of his sermon is better than thousands of our own prayers. (Walter Trobisch, *Martin Luther's Quiet Time* [Downers Grove, Ill.: InterVarsity Press, 1975], p. 14)

Approach, Study, Reflect

Spend time leisurely working through Psalm 34 today. In contrast to the other days, don't determine to get through the whole psalm. Although, if you do, that is fine too.

As I meditate through Psalm 34 today, I spend time on what it means to "taste and see that the Lord is good." First, I reflect on what it means to taste that the Lord is good. To taste is to experience a sensation. A good taste is a powerful experience. Just think about the times we should say no to a second helping and don't!

Second, I consider what it means to *see* that the Lord is good. It is one thing to be told about a person, "You will really like Bill." But it is completely different to meet that person for yourself.

Third, I reflect on what it means that the Lord *is* good. This may be shocking to you, but I struggle occasionally to believe that the Lord is good! Personal misfortunes and the pains of close friends raise specters of doubts.

I also stop to spend some time on verse 18, "The LORD is close to the brokenhearted and saves those who are crushed in spirit." I am feeling that way this week. I spend time here, turning away from my need to be self-righteous and victorious in my circumstances. I enter in to the knowledge that he is close to me in this very painful circumstance.

Now work through Psalm 34 for yourself.

Pray

Ask God to meet with you today. Tell him that fellowship with him is what is most important to you in life. (If that is not true, confess it to him and ask him to set your heart in the right direction.)

DAY 14

Acting on What We Know

Hear now, O Israel, the decrees and laws I am about to teach you. Follow them so that you may live and may go in and take possession of the land that the LORD, the God of your fathers, is giving you. Do not add to what I command you and do not subtract from it, but keep the commands of the LORD your God that I give you. (Deut 4:1-2)

God's Word always requires a response from us. To hear and not act is spiritual suicide. All during this week you have been responding in worship and appreciation. But as we encounter God in his Word, we must seek to act on it in ways that affect our own lives and the lives of others.

"What do the Scriptures principally teach? The Scriptures teach what man is to believe concerning God and what duty God requires from man" (*The Westminster Confession of Faith,* The Larger Catechism, Q. 5).

Study

Read through all of Psalm 34, noting what God requires of you (in what you say, how you think, and so on).

Reflect

Respond to the Lord in public praise.

In the first three verses there are different ways in which David praises the Lord. The Lord's praise is on his lips, rises from his soul and then expresses itself in calling others to praise the Lord.

When God does something for me, I tend to keep it to myself. I feel like it is overbearing to rush up to a friend and say, "Let me tell you what God just did for me."

But I have determined today that the small financial mess that I have been seeking God to deliver me from, and which has just been cleaned up, is something that God has done for me, and I will share my praise of God with a friend.

How will you respond to the Lord through public praise?

Respond to the Lord by asking for help.

David is able to seek God for help and not feel a need to be totally self-reliant. I value self-reliance too highly. I feel there is something wrong with me if I need to call on someone bigger than me. (I wouldn't get help from my older brothers when I was a child, and there were bullies in the neighborhood.) But I determine to seek the Lord's help first, and not only as a last resort.

How will you respond by asking for help?

Respond to the Lord by choosing obedience.

There is an ethical component to relying on the Lord. In verse 13 David calls on us to keep our tongues from evil, to seek peace, and to pursue it. I haven't done anything evil that I am conscious of, but I take this as a reinforcement to live in a way that is pleasing to God under the righteous authority of his Word.

How will you respond by choosing obedience?

What else will you do because of your time spent meditating on Psalm 34?

Pray

Ask God to make you obedient, dependent and grateful.

WEEK 3

Meditating on Life

I cried out to God for help;
  I cried out to God to hear me.
When I was in distress, I sought the Lord;
  at night I stretched out untiring hands
  and my soul refused to be comforted.

I remember you, O God, and I groaned;
  I mused, and my spirit grew faint.

You kept my eyes from closing;
  I was too troubled to speak.
I thought about the former days,
  the years of long ago;
I remembered my songs in the night.
  My heart mused and my spirit inquired:

"Will the LORD reject us forever?
  Will he never show his favor again?
Has his unfailing love vanished forever?
  Has his promise failed for all time?
Has God forgotten to be merciful?
  Has he in anger withheld his compassion?"

Then I thought, "To this I will appeal:
  the years of the right hand of the Most High."
I will remember the deeds of the LORD;
  yes, I will remember your miracles of long ago.
I will meditate on all your works
  and consider all your mighty deeds. (Ps 77:1-12)

DAY 15

Discerning God's Presence

I will meditate on all your works
and consider all your mighty deeds. (Ps 77:12)

When we lift our eyes from the pages of Scripture to go about the rest of our lives, it can be difficult to make the transition from past events to present spiritual truth. What does the crossing of the Red Sea, King David running from Saul, or the apostle Paul's struggle with the circumcision group have to do with life in the modern world? Where is God?

Our natural spiritual dullness is enhanced because we live in a culture which is committed to living in the absence of God. Even though, in principle, we believe in our Lord Jesus Christ as the Lord of all of life, we can find it difficult to live with his abiding presence.

That is why we must not only meditate on Scripture, but we must meditate on life as well. If we look with the eyes of faith and the guidance of the Scriptures, we will discern God's hand, guiding, teaching and shaping us.

However, before we can discern his presence in our lives in the present, we need to be able to take a long look at his hand in the past events of our lives. It is a principle of Scripture that *we must see the present through the experiences of the past.*

Study

As we prepare to meditate on life, let's look at God's unseen, guiding hand in the life of Joseph in Genesis 37—45.

Read Genesis 37. What is Joseph like?

What are his brothers like?

Joseph goes through years of pain. He spends time as an Egyptian slave (chapter 39) and then, by treachery of his master's wife, is thrown into prison, where he spends several years (chapter 40). Eventually he is delivered from prison and then ends up as a high official in Egypt, preparing Egypt to cope with a seven-year famine (chapters 40—41). Because of the widespread famine that affects the entire Middle East, Joseph's brothers come to buy grain from Egypt (Gen 42—45).

Against this background, look at Genesis 50:20. In your own words write down what Joseph is saying to his brothers.

Reflect

In many ways Genesis 50:20 is the climax of Joseph's life. He attributes all the painful events of his life to God's hand which was working for good. Make a list of major events in your life, both painful and pleasurable.

Now ask yourself, how do I see God's hand?

Close this time by reflecting briefly on Romans 8:28: "And we know that in all things God works for the good of those who love him, who have been called according to his purpose."

Pray

Ask God to show himself to you in the your daily tasks.

DAY 16

Remembering What God Has Done

So I will always remind you of these things, even though you know them and are firmly established in the truth you now have. I think it is right to refresh your memory. . . . And I will make every effort to see that after my departure you will always be able to remember these things. (2 Pet 1:12-15)

Spiritual truth is a slippery thing. Much of our task of knowing God is not learning new truth, but of keeping fresh what we already know. For this reason Moses admonished Israel, "Only be careful, and watch yourselves closely so that you do not forget the things your eyes have seen or let them slip from your heart as long as you live" (Deut 4:9).

What seems certain to us can fade into a vague unreality over the course of weeks, months and years. Keeping the truths of Scripture in our hearts can be like trying to walk up an escalator that is going down. We need to keep walking to make any headway, and if we stand still, we lose ground. That is one reason it is important to keep reading Scripture.

Psalm 105:1 says, "Give thanks to the LORD, call on his name; make known among the nations what he has done." The call to remember what God has done is all through the Scriptures. Psalms 77—78 and 104—106 are particular exercises of meditating on what God has done for Israel.

Study

Take a few minutes to read Psalm 77. Jot down benefits that come from remembering what God has done.

Reflect

Make a list of Christian truths that you need to recall (such as, God's forgiveness through the cross, your spiritual rebirth through the Spirit, the promise of heaven that awaits you).

Meditate on a couple of them that you think are particularly important to you right now. Be sure to enter into what you focus on. For instance see yourself being forgiven, see yourself entering heaven. Use your mind, your emotions and your senses.

Close this time by briefly reflecting on 2 Timothy 3:16-17: "All Scripture is God-breathed and is useful for teaching, rebuking, correcting and training in righteousness, so that the man of God may be thoroughly equipped for every good work."

Pray

Ask God to keep his truth alive in your heart.

DAY 17

Recovering Our Emotions

And now, O Israel, what does the LORD your God ask of you
but to fear the LORD your God, to walk in all his ways, to love him,
to serve the LORD your God with all your heart and
with all your soul? (Deut 10:12)

Before we can be free to meditate on the Lord's presence in our lives we need to be in touch with our emotions.

Some of us have been warned to avoid looking for any feelings when we have a quiet time. Certainly there is wisdom in this caution because there is more to knowing God than mere feelings. But we miss something important when we seek wrongly to suppress or control our emotions. I do a good deal of counseling and more often than not, I find that the source of great inward conflict that flows out into unhealthy behavior comes from suppressed emotions.

Emotions are an important part of our life. They are the engines which motivate us. Take away all our emotions, and we end up being dull and lifeless. And emotions are especially important in our relationship with God.

Jonathan Edwards writes:

> That religion which God requires, and will accept, does not consist in weak, dull and lifeless wishes, raising us but a little above a state of indifference; God, in his word, greatly insists upon it, that we be in good earnest, fervent in spirit; and our hearts vigorously engaged in religion. (Jonathan Edwards, *Religious Affections,* p. 27)

So, we must rethink our emotions. We must value them and seek to get in touch with them. Depending on a number of factors, some of us are more in touch with our emotions than others.

Approach

God is the source of love. Sit back and allow him to put his arms around you. Write down how you respond emotionally.

Study

Let's look at some of the emotions mentioned in Scripture that Edwards chronicles in *Religious Affections.* Summarize each verse in a sentence or two.

Fear: "But the eyes of the Lord are on those who fear him, on those whose hope is in his unfailing love" (Ps 33:18).

"The fear of the Lord is the beginning of knowledge, but fools despise wisdom and discipline" (Prov 1:8).

Hate: "To fear the LORD is to hate evil; I hate pride and arrogance, evil behavior and perverse speech" (Prov 8:13).

"I hate those who cling to worthless idols; I trust in the LORD" (Ps 31:6).

Sorrow: "Blessed are those who mourn, for they will be comforted" (Mt 5:4).

"The LORD is close to the brokenhearted and saves those who are crushed in spirit" (Ps 34:18).

Joy: "Delight yourself in the LORD and he will give you the desires of your heart" (Ps 37:4).

"Rejoice in the Lord always. I will say it again: Rejoice!" (Phil 4:4).

Reflect

There are lots of other emotions that could be named. Spend some time now writing down emotions that you discover as you face the incidents of your life.

What are you struggling with right now? How does it make you feel?

What is there is your life to be glad about? What emotions can you discern?

What is there about God right now that stirs your emotions?

Pray

Seek God to fill you with a desire for him.

Ask God to give you a joy in him that overflows into the life of others.

DAY 18

Understanding Emotional Cycles

You turned my wailing into dancing;
you removed my sackcloth and clothed me with joy,
that my heart may sing to you and not be silent.
O LORD my god, I will give you thanks forever. (Ps 30:11-12)

If we are to live with our emotions, we must face emotional swings. We can go from the heights of joy in God to the depths of despair, all in the same day.

When I was a new believer, I was told that emotional swings were normal for those who were spiritually immature. As I got older, I was supposed to grow beyond those swings into a stable plane of emotional maturity.

That, however, is not what I have discovered. My emotions, if anything, have grown more intense. As my heart was strengthened in the Spirit and the Word, my emotions came more and more into play.

If we are to grow in the inner life that allows us to meditate on life, we must face the emotional swings.

In our quiet time today, we look at two potential extremes of our emotional swings—despair and joy.

Despair is a threatening emotion. Turned inward it takes the form of paralyzing depression. Uncontrolled and allowed to grow it can lead us to a lonely isolation from others. And it can become a sooty dark cloud that obscures God from our sight. Because despair is so threatening we tend to ignore, suppress, or run from it whenever we might have to face it. The problem of course is that it doesn't go away. It broods and grows in the depths of our hearts.

Joy is a thrill and pleasure that lifts us to the heights. Yet joy, like despair, is a messy emotion. It causes us to walk around smiling, singing and patting people on the back. Others who come near in our times of joy are likely to respond: "What has got in to you?"

For this reason, we may tend to avoid joy (particularly joy in God), or at least harness and control it. If we get too excited about God, we are likely to hear, "Don't get so carried away."

But when we do harness joy, it's like popping a balloon. The uplifting joy is squeezed out, leaving us deflated and flat.

Study

Read Psalm 31:9-24 which tells about David's emotional swings. What emotional words does David use to describe his situation in verses 9-13?

What seems to be a primary cause of his grief?

What requests does David make of God in verses 14-18?

What emotions do you think he was feeling as he called out to God?

David moves from distress to praise in verses 19-24. What does David appreciate about God?

How does his relief and joy in God affect him?

Reflect

Consider emotional swings in your life. See if you can recall a couple of swings that you have recently experienced. Write down what happened and how you felt. (It is important that you be honest and identify the feelings of pain as well as feelings of pleasure.)

What did God have to do in all of this?

DAY 19

Meditating on the Past

Praise the LORD, O my soul;
all my inmost being, praise his holy name.
Praise the LORD, O my soul,
and forget not all his benefits. (Ps 103:1-2)

Now it is time to begin to pull together emotions, memory and the presence of God.

Remembrance of what God has done is the life blood of spiritual health. It is the spring of joy and gratitude. As Israel looked back to the Exodus and deliverance from slavery, we look back to the cross and the deliverance from bondage to sin and Satan.

The problem for us is that when we go through day-by-day tasks of life, what God has said and done can seem dated and old. As clothes wear out and fashions change, as the new car becomes used and broken, we can think that God's actions and words become outdated and need to be repaired or updated.

However God's truth and actions are eternal. God's speaking and actions are not merely isolated events, they continue on forever. If God says he loves us, he always loves us. If God says we are forgiven, then we are always forgiven.

Day by day God is meeting us and speaking to us. However, there are times when he seems silent. During those times we need to look back. Back to his Word and back to the times that he has graced us with his help and presence.

Reflect

Today, we are going to consider the events of our lives for the past six months to a year. In the left-hand column of the chart on page 67 entitled "Events," list *events and experiences or major issues* that you have faced in the last six to twelve months. The list doesn't have to be in any special order. Just use one or two words that remind you of things you can recall. Don't look for things that are necessarily "spiritual," just things that have happened.

The middle column, entitled "Emotions," is for you to consider your emotional responses to each event you have listed in the first column. In just a word or two write down your emotions as you can recall them (satisfied, disappointed, pleased, upset and so on).

The third column entitled "Perceptions" is to help you ponder what God is doing in your life. Look over all that you have written in the "Events" and "Emotions" columns, and see if you can see ways that God has been working. Do you see any common themes or patterns? Is there an inner conviction that God has been working in you or through you?

Meditating on the Past **Recent Events, Emotions and Perceptions**		
Events List events, experiences and issues that come to mind.	**Emotions** Write down emotions that accompany your list of events.	**Perceptions** Write down any themes or patterns that you can discern.

What do you think the Lord is doing in your life?

After you have worked through your recent past, sit in quiet appreciation for God's persistent faithful work in your life.

Pray

You may have glimpsed ways in which you have not been responsive to God's work. It might be appropriate to spend time in repentance. You may have glimpsed ways in which God has been abundantly good to you, ways in which you have just not seen before. It may be appropriate to spend time in thanksgiving.

Take time now to "Give him the glory due his name."

DAY 20

Meditating on the Present

The Lord is my shepherd, I shall lack nothing.
He makes me lie down in green pastures,
he leads me beside quiet waters,
he restores my soul.
He guides me in paths of righteousness
for his name's sake. (Ps 23:1-3)

Today, we turn our eyes from the past to the present.

God has been working to bring us to where we are today. Once we have a glimpse of what he has been doing, it is easier to see the ways in which he is involved with us daily.

As God works in our lives, he requires us to respond. It may be that as you look at your week you will see that you are frequently in situations in which you are having to ask forgiveness of others. In this case it may be that God is calling you to practice humility. Or it may be that you are confronted with a series of crises in which others were let down by you. Perhaps, then, God is requiring you to be more responsible to others.

I went through a week recently in which I was running into a series of financial problems from seemingly unrelated directions. After the third such problem in a week, it became clear that there was something more than just money involved. After discussion and prayer with my wife, Jackie, I came to the conclusion that God was confronting me on some poor decisions and wrong attitudes. First, I felt called to repent. Then I determined with Jackie ways that I could be more carefully disciplined in what we spent as a family.

Reflect

Today, we will make a list of what has happened in the *past week*. There is a new element in the "Perceptions" column of the chart that will help you to respond to God. You are to consider what God is asking you to do.

Meditating on the Present This Week's Events, Emotions and Perceptions		
Events List events, experiences and issues that come to mind.	**Emotions** Write down emotions that may have been created by the things on your list.	**Perceptions** Write down any themes or patterns that you can discern. What do you think the Lord is asking you to do?

Pray

Ask God to give you the faith and courage to do what he wants you to do.

DAY 21

Meditating on the Future

Blessed are you who hunger now,
for you will be satisfied.
Blessed are you who weep now,
for you will laugh. (Lk 6:21)

We have meditated on the past and the present, it is now time to meditate on the future.

A prayer of Moses says, "Teach us to number our days aright, that we may gain a heart of wisdom" (Ps 90:12). When we think of the future, we often think in terms of guidance. Asking questions like, "What does God want us to do in the next five or ten years?" But we should know that such a way of thinking about the future is new, something that we modern Christians are so taken up with.

From the New Testament times on, Christians thought of the future, not as what we will do in this life, but in the life that is coming when Christ returns. The apostle Paul bids us: "Set your minds on things above, not on earthly things. For you died, and your life is now hidden with Christ in God. When Christ, who is your life, appears, then you also will appear with him in glory" (Col 3:2-4).

And Thomas à Kempis writes, "what peace and inward quiet should he have who would cut away from himself all busyness of mind, and think only on heavenly things" (Thomas à Kempis, *Imitation).*

Let's bring these two perspectives together, and consider the need for guidance in the immediate future with our ultimate future in the heavenly kingdom.

Reflect

Under "Events" list things that you would like to accomplish in the next five years. Under "Emotions" list why you desire these things. And under "Perceptions" respond to the three questions.

Meditating on the Future Events, Emotions and Perceptions for Five Years		
Events List the things you want to accomplish in the next 5-10 years.	**Emotions** Write down why you want to accomplish these things.	**Perceptions** How do your goals advance the kingdom of heaven in this world? How will your desire find completion when Jesus returns? What do you think that the Lord is asking you to do?

Pray

Ask God to fill you with a sense of hope for his coming.

Ask him to use you to proclaim the good news of Jesus' return.

WEEK 4

Praying

Out of the depths I cry to you, O LORD;
O Lord, hear my voice.
Let your ears be attentive
to my cry for mercy.

If you, O LORD, kept a record of sins,
O Lord, who could stand?
But with you there is forgiveness;
therefore you are feared.

I wait for the LORD, my soul waits,
and in his word I put my hope.
My soul waits for the Lord
more than watchmen wait for the morning,
more than watchmen wait for the morning.

O Israel, put your hope in the LORD,
for with the LORD is unfailing love
and with him is full redemption.
He himself will redeem Israel
from all their sins. (Ps 130)

DAY 22

Learning How to Pray

Hear my cry, O God;
listen to my prayer. (Ps 61:1)

Prayer is the pinnacle of spiritual life. One of the greatest privileges we can have is to ask God to do something and see him do it!

Prayer is very simple, but amazingly difficult. It is something a newborn babe in Christ can do from the very first. Yet it is also something that the greatest saints must still learn.

It is at this level of my relationship with God that I constantly struggle. I can spend time in silence and solitude. I can be content in a restful peace in the Lord's presence. But when I move to prayer, biblical prayer, I wrestle.

Prayer can be defined broadly as "communion with God." Or it can be narrowly and biblically defined as *"asking God for help."* Look through the prayers of the Bible and that is what you will find—Abraham seeking a son, David crying out for deliverance from his enemies, Nehemiah asking for help in rebuilding Jerusalem. All God's people come to him with problems or needs and ask for help.

Then why is prayer so hard, so confusing and so threatening? After all, what is difficult about asking God to do something? You just open your mouth and tell God what you need.

But it is not that easy to do, is it? A thousand questions come to mind, plus objections, reservations, hesitations. How should we approach God? What should we say? How should we say it? What right do we have to ask God for anything? How do we know that he will answer? How can the eternal God listen to our small concerns?

I don't have an answer to all these questions. However, as we go through this week together, I invite you to enter into my struggle.

Approach

Place yourself, actually or in your mind's eye, on your knees before God. Acknowledge that you need his help to live. Sit or kneel until you can rest in your sense of dependence. Write down how you feel about being dependent.

Reflect

Spend some time evaluating your ability to pray. Can you ask God for help? Why or why not?

How often do you pray?

What do you ask God for?

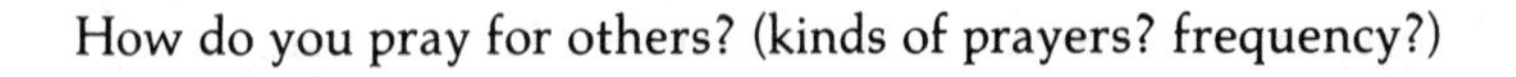

How do you pray for others? (kinds of prayers? frequency?)

How do you feel when you pray?

Do you see answers to your prayers? Explain.

What other problems with or questions about prayer do you have?

Pray

The disciples expressed their inadequacy when they approached Jesus with their request, "Lord, teach us to pray" (Lk 11:1-4). The first disciples needed to be taught, and so do we. Consider how you resist the Lord in prayer. Then spend a few minutes asking the Lord to teach you to pray.

DAY 23

Making a List

And I will do whatever you ask in my name, so that the Son may bring glory to the Father. You may ask me for anything in my name, and I will do it. (Jn 14:13-14)

"Aim at nothing and you are sure to hit it," goes the old saying. If we don't have a list, our prayers will probably be wandering, unfocused and haphazard.

I am not particularly disciplined and developing a prayer list that I use day after day is something I tend to avoid. I go through phases when I don't use one. But I am using one currently and experiencing some very satisfying times of intercession. Despite my fears of getting caught in empty religious repetition, I am convinced that a list is the best way to go about regular prayers.

Just opening my notebook with my prayer list and placing it on my desk helps me be settled and consistent. And there is something about it that focuses my wandering thoughts. Through the daily practice of using it, my whole being knows it's time to settle down and do business with God.

A prayer list can be as sophisticated as index cards with pictures of people you pray for, or it can be merely a sheet of paper that you have jotted words on. The first couple of pages in the front of my journal is where I put names of people I am praying for or a brief description of issues I am concerned about. As my prayers are answered, I put a check mark and a date by my request.

There are two extremes to avoid in making a list. You don't want it to be too general or too specific.

General Prayers

We can sweep over issues for prayer with a broad wave. "God please help my friend, Bill," or "Please help me to do better today." Such prayers can be merely an attempt to do our religious duty without extending ourselves or engaging God.

But not all general prayers are bad. The Lord's prayer is a prayer list that is quite broad. The petitions are brief and cover all our basic needs in just a few sentences. The clear simplicity of them helps us focus on what is essential.

Specific Prayers

The general needs covered in the Lord's Prayer express themselves in our lives in specific ways. Our need for daily bread may be expressed in balancing our bank account or seeking a raise. Forgiveness of sins may mean asking for forgiveness for harboring anger towards your spouse or friend. Deliverance from temptation may require keeping a chaste attitude toward someone at work or not fudging on the expense account.

Taking your cues from the Lord's Prayer, your specific requests need not be detailed. Tell God what you want. Don't say it over and over. Don't elaborate. Just tell him. Pray for one entry on your list, then move on to the next.

But be careful as you pray. In contrast to being too general, we can become so specific that we clutter our prayers and cloud up what we are really seeking from God.

Pray

There are two columns on the worksheet for today. One is for the Lord's Prayer and one is for your specific petitions. Spend time in prayer, first praying through the Lord's Prayer. Then, as you pray, list in the right-hand column issues and concerns that you need to be seeking God about.

Prayer List

Learning to Pray Broadly	**Learning to Pray Specifically**
Our Father (Embracing our relationship)	Things I want God to do.
Hallowed be your name (Petition of worship)	Family
Your kingdom come (Petition for mission)	Friends
Give us our daily bread (Petition for sustenance)	Issues/Concerns
Forgive our sins (Petition for mercy)	
Lead us not into temptation (Petition for protection)	

DAY 24

Praying in Need

Save me, O God,
for the waters have come up to my neck.
I sink in the miry depths. . . .
I am worn out calling for help;
my throat is parched.
My eyes fail,
looking for my God. (Ps 69:1-3)

I slammed my fist on the steering wheel and said, "God, if you don't help us, we are going to be in big trouble!"

The source of this outburst was family conflict. I left the house that morning in a state of turmoil. Jackie and I had a long-standing disagreement, and it had erupted into an exchange of sharp words. I had been praying casually about our differences over the past month, but this morning I felt desperate.

After my outburst to God, there was a sense of peace in the car. It was almost as if I heard a voice. "Now you are serious about your request, and now I will answer you."

And the prayer was answered. Jackie and I were able, within the next week, to sort out significant differences.

Prayers grow out of our need for God and his help. Although he answers all kinds of prayer, it is clear from the Scriptures that God is most inclined toward prayer that grows from our heartfelt urgency and desire. For instance, the Holy Spirit, who has been given to help us pray, "intercedes for us with groans that words cannot express" (Rom 8:26).

When we pray, and especially when we pray through our prayer list, it is possible to slip into a casual passiveness, "God do this, and this and this, and (yawn), don't forget that as well." Instead, when we pray, we should seek God for our needs with a deep, even yearning, sense of need.

Approach
Imagine that you are in a desert and in need of water. You see a well in the distance and head for it. How do you feel? Now see your heart as the desert and the Lord as the well. Write down your responses.

Study
Let's look at the attitude of prayer from the Scriptures. Read Psalm 130:1-2. Which words express emotion?

Describe the attitude of the psalmist.

When have you approached God with such an attitude?

How is it possible to approach God with such a sense of need about your prayers as a way of life?

Read verses 3-4. Why do you think that the psalmist confesses sin as he appeals to God?

Read verses 5-6. What do you observe about the psalmist as he waits for the Lord?

Reflect

It is possible to harbor the thought that God is obliged to answer our prayers. However, in verses 3-4, the psalmist renounces any appearance of a demanding attitude. How do you respond to unanswered prayers? (For instance, are you angry when you don't get what you ask for?)

In verses 5-6 we saw the psalmist is waiting and hoping for the Lord, not passively, but actively—"more than the watchmen wait for the morning." How well do your prayers reflect this active anticipation of a watchman waiting for the morning?

How is God responding to your prayers?

Pray

Now work through your prayer list. Linger over each entry and seek to cultivate a sense of dependency and need.

DAY 25

Praying Right

If I had cherished sin in my heart,
the Lord would not have listened;
but God has surely listened
and heard my voice in prayer.
Praise be to God,
who has not rejected my prayer
or withheld his love from me! (Ps 66:18-20)

We should expect to get answers to our prayers. Otherwise, praying is merely a pious game. Richard Foster goes so far as to write, "We can determine if we are praying aright if the requests come to pass" (Richard Foster, *Celebration).*

Initially I found this idea unsettling. Were all my prayers supposed to be answered? Was it possible that I was not praying right?

I still have some questions about such a sense of certainty for answered prayer. But in struggling with answered and unanswered prayer, I became convinced that I had much to learn about prayer. I did see that getting answers to prayers comes from learning to pray. And I did discover that answered prayer has conditions.

The condition of answered prayer is not a mystery.

It is simply laid out by Jesus in John 14:14, "You may ask me for anything in my name, and I will do it."

In My Name

To understand this promise of answered prayer, we must keep in mind the original context. Jesus was about to depart to heaven. The disciples were about to be sent on a lifelong mission. And they were all stressed. How could they carry on the work of the kingdom of God without

Jesus? The assuring answer was prayer. For the work which Jesus assigned them, they could ask for what they needed and be assured that they would receive it. But they had to ask, in Jesus' name.

Now what does it mean to pray in the name of Jesus? Perhaps an illustration will help. I used to have an expense account for the cost of my ministry with InterVarsity Christian Fellowship. It wasn't my money; it was InterVarsity's. But I was authorized to use it for whatever I needed, as long as it furthered the ministry. When I traveled to a campus or a conference or bought anything that I used for ministry, I didn't have to take it out of my family's income. Another way to say this is, I spent money in the name of InterVarsity.

Having an expense account gave me a great deal of freedom. I didn't have to worry about money for mailing letters, traveling, photocopying and so on. As long as the expense was for ministry, I could draw on the account.

But the expense account had conditions. I had to keep in mind that it was not my money. I couldn't use it for my personal benefit. For instance, I couldn't put my family in the car and take a trip for a couple of days' vacation and use my InterVarsity account to pay for it.

This promise of prayer in Jesus' name is similar, though not exactly the same. Our Lord promises the resources we need as we serve him. All we need to do is ask. This means that we can have great confidence and freedom. There are supernatural resources available to us. The condition for getting the help from heaven is that we must ask for things, in his name, according to the purpose of the mission.

Praying in Jesus' name is not the same as my expense account since the purposes of his mission are not limited to official ministry. Much of what we might think of as personal needs also fit into the kingdom of God. I can ask, in the name of Jesus, for my personal needs and the needs of family and friends.

But we must be careful here. Even when we ask for personal needs, we must keep in mind that the whole focus of our lives is not for personal gratification but obedience to the will of our Lord. As Jesus prayed in the Garden of Gethsemane, "not my will but yours be done" (Lk 22:42).

This way of praying transforms us. It reshapes our thinking about ourselves and all of life. It turns us away from self-centeredness. We don't serve ourselves, we serve the Lord. We pray and we live, in Jesus' name.

Approach

Spend the first part of today's quiet time settling before the Lord. Ask him to focus your heart on his will for you and for those around you. As you find distractions coming in, turn them over to the Lord.

Pray

Now, work through your prayer list for today. Appeal for each request on the basis of how it conforms to the kingdom of God.

DAY 26

Knowing What to Ask

In the same way, the Spirit helps us in our weakness. We do not know what we ought to pray, but the Spirit himself intercedes for us with groans that words cannot express. And he who searches our hearts knows the mind of the Spirit, because the Spirit intercedes for the saints in accordance with God's will. (Rom 8:26-27)

An important part of praying in a way that receives answers from God is listening to the Spirit so that he can tell us what to pray for.

Several years ago a good friend of mine was considering a job change, and he asked me to pray. Initially, I prayed a general prayer. I asked God to give him wisdom about what he should do. But I didn't say anything to him or God about what I thought best; I wasn't sure.

After several weeks of praying, I became deeply convinced that he should not take the position. I began praying that he would refuse it. Shortly after that decision, I received a letter saying that he had turned it down. He and his wife had come to the conclusion that a change in careers was not right for God's call on their life or for the health of their family.

I confess that I have a tendency to be skeptical. When I first began to pay attention to such inner inclinations, I was not sure whether they were fantasies of my creative mind or actually guidance from the Spirit. After seeing answers like this once or twice, I became more convinced that God was giving specific wisdom and then answering the prayers.

Recognizing Wisdom

We must pay attention to our heart responses, as well as to what we think is best. By doing so, you will notice that inwardly you respond to your prayer items in a variety of ways.

Some people or things that you pray for will have a sense of urgency about them. Respond by calling out to God with a deep sense of inner desire. Or, you may notice that for some people there is a kind of blank. I find that there are some issues and people that I can't seem to bring into focus in my mind's eye. In such cases, I pray a very general prayer and wait to see if I am given further direction over the next several weeks. For others there can be a heaviness. Praying for them is like trying to lift a huge weight. For these, too, I pray a general prayer and listen to see what guidance I will be given.

For some items you pray for, it may seem that there is a clear sense of logic about what you should ask God for. Looking at the issues, a certain course just makes sense. Have the courage to ask God for this too.

Pray boldly. If you are praying for something improperly, asking for the wrong thing, or asking without faith, ask God to show you. He will.

Approach

Think about your family, friends, work, church, any and every area of your life. Turn everything over to him. What difference does it make in the way you live to see these as a calling from him?

Study

The issue of listening to God and praying as you feel led is really a matter of wisdom. Read James 1:2-6 (note especially verse 5). In your own words, try to define the word *wisdom.*

Write down what is necessary in order to receive wisdom from God.

We can be sure that if we ask and listen, God will give us wisdom about how to pray. Applied to prayer, wisdom is knowing the best thing to pray for.

Pray

Ask God for wisdom for each of the items on your list. Spend some time in quiet just listening. Pray as you believe you are being guided by God's Spirit.

Take time to pray through your list too.

DAY 27

Persisting in Prayer

Give us each day our daily bread. (Lk 11:3)

Praying for something once is seldom enough. We must pray repeatedly until we sense that God says no, or until he answers our prayer.

Now that you have prayed through your list several times, you may be wondering what else you need to pray for. Be careful about adding to your list too quickly. You are just getting started praying for what you already have on it.

I tend to think that if I have spoken to God about something once that is enough. After all, God knows my needs anyway. Or if I must pray more than once, then I hoped that if I mention my concerns to him a couple of times a week, that will do the trick.

But over the years I have discovered that it is the things that I repeatedly call out to the Lord for on a daily basis which get an answer.

It makes sense when you think about it. One of God's requirements for prayer is a sense of need. If I am not interested enough to call out to God on a daily basis, then I must not be very needy. In that case I can't expect him take me too seriously.

There are some things that must be prayed for every day all our lives. Other things need to be prayed for daily until they are answered.

Lifelong Prayers

According to our Lord, we need to pray daily for the coming of his kingdom. And we need to seek daily bread, as well as forgiveness and deliverance from temptation.

Praying for these things daily is a great spiritual work. First, God provides for the coming of his kingdom through our prayers. Things happen all over the world and in eternity when we ask this. This is a great mystery, nevertheless it is true.

Second, God provides for our needs and protection as well as those of others through our praying his prayer daily. If this need for protection and provision is not obvious, it is because we live in a secularized culture that would have us think that we can get on in life without any help from God. But beware—unless you pray for provision, protection and forgiveness, you will be living an impoverished life and yet be blind to the very poverty you experience.

Until They Are Answered

Your faith will grow as you see answers and begin crossing things off your list. God answers prayers all the time, but we often miss this because we aren't looking. When you pray daily and keep a list, you will be much more inclined to recognize answers when they come.

Additionally, as you pray daily, you will find that your prayers become sharpened. As I pray through my list of friends, I start off generally asking God's blessing. But over the weeks I learn about problems at home, a deep hurt from years past, or a major crisis at work, that need God's help. And as I pray with more insight for needs, there is a growing experience of God's loving power.

Approach

What unanswered prayers have you sought the Lord for? Write down how you feel: frustrated, angry, sad, indifferent. Once you have done that give your prayers and your feelings over to the Lord.

Study

Read the parable of the persistent widow in Luke 18:1-8. Write out what you perceive to be Jesus' point.

Pray

Remind yourself, as you turn to your prayer list, that this daily routine is more than an empty ritual. Have clearly in mind that you and the people you pray for desperately need God's help. Seeking God is not optional for those who would know spiritual life.

Now pray through your list. Begin to listen for ways in which the Lord might be sharpening your prayers.

If you have already recognized answers to prayer, put a big checkmark by them, and give thanks to God.

DAY 28

Waiting in Prayer

I waited patiently for the LORD;
he turned to me and heard my cry.
He lifted me out of the slimy pit,
out of the mud and mire;
he set my feet on a rock
and gave me a firm place to stand. (Ps 40:1-3)

I hate waiting.

But those who pray must learn to wait. Sometimes we must wait months. Sometimes we must wait years. And waiting a long time can be discouraging.

I wonder what it must have been like for Zechariah, the father of John the Baptist, when the angel showed up in the temple and announced that his prayers had been answered: "Do not be afraid, Zechariah; your prayer has been heard. Your wife Elizabeth will bear you a son, and you are to give him the name John" (Lk 1:13).

By the time the angel showed up Zechariah and Elizabeth were very old, far beyond the child-bearing years. Surely they had given up praying for children long before. Zechariah must have wondered, "What prayers?"

Waiting on the Lord takes us to the heart of prayer. When we wait, we are reminded that God works according to his time, not our convenience. When we wait, we are placed in a position of humility. Waiting puts us in the right place before God, longing for him to hear us and respond. When we wait, there is eager expectation like a child as Christmas approaches. "Dad, how much longer to Christmas?" "Can we just open one present a little early?"

Isaiah writes, "They that wait upon the Lord," and in one version the word *wait* is translated as "hope." As Isaiah writes: "But those who hope in the LORD will renew their strength. They will soar on wings like eagles; they will run and not grow weary, they will walk and not be faint" (Isa 40:31).

God not only gives us what we ask for as we wait on him, he meets our needs. (Sometimes what we need and what we ask for are very different.) We receive a refreshment of soul and body when we wait. When I sit quietly and expectantly before the Lord in prayer, I sense the room filled with a restoring fullness that is cleansing and renewing.

Approach

Imagine that you have been lost in forest during the winter. After wandering for weeks, your food is gone, you are cold and lonely. Just when you have given up hope, the rescue party comes. They pick you up, give you warm clothes, feed you, and then put you in a car and begin driving you home. What would you feel like during the drive back to your friends and family?

Study

Read through these scriptures on waiting:

Wait for the LORD;
  be strong and take heart
  and wait for the LORD. (Ps 27:14)

I wait for the LORD, my soul waits,
  and in his word I put my hope. (Ps 130:5)

Yet the LORD longs to be gracious to you;
he rises to show you compassion.
For the LORD is a God of justice.
Blessed are all who wait for him! (Is 30:18)

The creation waits in eager expectation for the sons of God to be revealed. (Rom 8:19)

Not only so, but we ourselves, who have the firstfruits of the Spirit, groan inwardly as we wait eagerly for our adoption as sons, the redemption of our bodies. (Rom 8:23)

What stands out to you?

What are we waiting for?

What are the benefits of waiting?

What do you need to learn about waiting?

Pray

As you pray through your list today, set your heart both to long for God to answer and to rest in the confidence that he will do what is best, in his time and in his way.

CONCLUSION

The Next Step

O God, you are my God,
earnestly I seek you;
my soul thirsts for you,
my body longs for you
in a dry and weary land
where there is no water. (Ps 63:1)

Now is the time to consider how your attitude toward your quiet times has been affected through these studies. What are you pleased about? In what areas would you like to improve?

You may also be wondering, "Where do I go from here?"

☐ To begin try using some of the exercises from week one on seeking God again. Or you might choose another psalm or short passage of Scripture and read over it for a week in study and meditation.

☐ Continue to look weekly or daily at the events of your life to discern the Lord's guiding hand.

☐ Pray with dependence and urgency. Pray the Lord's Prayer daily and intercede for the concerns he brings your way.

Variety

In each of the four weeks we've focused on different spiritual disciplines. Blending the spiritual exercises should give a good experience of variety, and this is important in a quiet time. I find that if I settle on one way for very long it dries up. Sometimes I focus on seeking God through silence and solitude, sometimes through in-depth Bible study and sometimes through intercessory prayer.

The goal is balance. Over a month or two, we need to spend time in warming up our hearts, in study and meditation and in prayer. To focus on one element for an extended period is not healthy. Imagine eating only steak for two months—or only fruit. It wouldn't be long before we would notice physical (and perhaps mental) health problems.

Scripture

Although all the disciplines are important, the Scriptures need to have the central place. They are the spectacles you see with (John Calvin's rich image). Unless you put them on, everything will be out of focus.

You will notice that study and meditation on Scripture were only dealt with in week two, yet the Scriptures were incorporated in some way every day. It is important to keep up the same pattern. Even if you choose to spend the majority of your time in intercessory prayer or in resting in the presence of the Lord, you need to read over portions of Scripture to direct your heart and mind in God's truth.

Persistence

And when you let your times with the Lord slip, start them up again.

My own quiet times seem to be a series of beginnings. Just recently, I went through a time of testing, and the Lord seemed absent. As I called out to God with an urgent plea for help, I sensed a quiet rebuke rising within me, "You aren't doing what you know."

In the crises of the last few months, I had let my quiet times lapse. The pressures of life had gotten in the way. A quick reading of a passage of Scripture and run through of my prayer list were the extent of my times with God. Of course God seemed distant. So, I turned back to a proper cultivation of spiritual disciplines that take the focus off myself and the world to a proper focus back on God and his Word. That in short, is what all spiritual exercises are about.

Further Help

If you found this guide helpful and you want to continue with guided quiet times, look for the other Spiritual Encounter Guides.